EARTHSONG

How To Design

A Truly Spectacular

Natural Garden

EARTHSONG

How To Design
A Truly Spectacular
Natural Garden

By
Chase Revel

LASERVISION, INC.
Publishing Division
Carson City, Nevada

Library of Congress Cataloging-in-Publication Data

Main entry under title:

Earthsong: how to design a truly spectacular
natural garden.

1. Gardens—Design—Addresses, essays, lectures.
2. Gardens—Addresses, essays, lectures. I. Revel, Chase.

ISBN 0-9638714-1-2

Printed and bound in Hong Kong.

10 9 8 7 6 5 4 3 2 1

Contents

Foreword: Philosophy Of Natural Garden Design

Imagine for a moment that you want to paint a beautiful landscape, but you have only minimal skills as an artist. Your next choice would be to find a good landscape artist and tell him or her exactly the way you want it to look.

Unfortunately, there are very few artists that have the talent for photographic realism. However, I happen to know the absolutely best one in the world that will not only create whatever you want, but will allow you to sign your name to the work because she will never ever tell.

All this artist requires is that you sketch crude shapes of the plants in the spots where you want them. Then dab a spot of each color appearing on each plant and in the background.

Give your rendition to this artist and within a few months to a year, she will give you an absolutely gorgeous infinitely detailed masterpiece—a painting so incredibly beautiful that the work of no artist, living or dead, even comes close. Best of all, you don't have to pay her.

She is very reliable. I know because I work with her regularly. I assemble the elements and put them where I think they should go. Then she takes over and does all the hard work like filling in the details, making everything flow together harmoniously and creating some very spectacular landscapes.

In this book, I'll show you how to best use her talents to make a garden masterpiece of your own. Her name is Mother Nature!

Introduction: No Straight Lines

For Mother Nature

Creating things with straight lines, balance and symmetry is natural for humans. Therefore, most gardens are planted with logical, straight-lined orderliness.

Mother Nature, on the other hand, has a laissez-faire attitude. She lets seeds fall to the ground where they may. Consequently, as we walk through the forests and fields planted naturally, we find the placement of trees, shrubs, flowers and grass random, disordered and asymmetrical.

Most humans have an affinity for nature, but in general we find it to be only somewhat aesthetically pleasing. Then there are times when walking through a monotonously common forest, we come upon a scene that is serenely or even awesomely beautiful.

In analyzing those rare, beautiful natural scenes, we find that there are few straight lines, if any, and no symmetry. How then, can a human create a garden as spectacular as Mother Nature's finest?

It is not as difficult as it may sound. There are some simple principles. In the following pages, I will show photos that illustrate how to create a sensational natural garden using the artistic side of your brain. However, throughout this book I will also satisfy your logical side with tips on the best plants and keeping the maintenance to a minimum.

Regardless of the level of your gardening expertise, you will be able to choose ideas from this book, easily execute them and soon be known for having a truly spectacular natural garden.

A microscene is a scene where you can view it in its entirety without moving your head or eyes. Try this exercise. Stand up and look down at a 45 degree angle. Although your peripheral vision allows you to see an area 20 to 30 feet wide, your clearest view from this angle is only about six to eight feet wide and approximately four to six feet deep.

That is the ideal size for a microscene, because it makes the person viewing it want to look at it longer. The reason is, ideally, there is nothing to draw one's attention out of the scene. Scenes can be smaller, but larger ones should be limited to those areas where people can see them from further away when the scene first comes into view.

There is no limitation to the number of microscenes you can have in your garden. In fact, the more you have, the more interesting and fascinating your garden becomes. The only restriction is that you should not put two small microscenes (smaller than four feet by four feet) side by side without at least six feet between them. That would be like an artist putting two different scenes on one painting.

Use A Variety Of Textures And Shapes

As you try to shed your linear, logical thought patterns to design microscenes, also you must stop the tendency to clump similar things together. By combining various textures, shapes and color tones as you see in the photo, more interest is created.

The ground cover, Baby Tears, *Helxine soleirolii* (zones 9 through 10), has been allowed to migrate up and over the stone planter wall, but it appears to be going the other way, overflowing from the planter. (For an explanation of zones, see page 53.)

Stumps Add Character To Microscenes

As a stump deteriorates, it presents many visual changes. First the bark dries, changes color, then splits and finally falls off. At each stage, the presentation harks of a deep misty forest scene—exactly what you want for your natural garden.

When the bark drops off, you can leave it there for its natural look, and as mulch. With the bark gone, the trunk will accelerate its transition and will go through many stages that are visually interesting before it is totally destroyed. Every type of tree deteriorates differently—each with its own character and distinct appearance.

In the photo, the moist porous bark of this stump has given the Baby Tears a nutritional stronghold providing a natural beauty no landscape designer could ever achieve. This illustrates what I mean when I say Mother Nature will fill in the details and do the fine brush strokes.

The concrete sculpture is flanked by perennial Impatiens (annuals in zones lower than nine), known as Bizzy Lizzies on the left and Sword Ferns, *Nephrolepis cordifolia* (zones 7 through 10), in front. River polished, black La Paz pebbles flow around the scene.

The redwood blocks are used to separate a slightly higher elevation from the lower one in front of the stump, but failed to contain the wandering Baby Tears.

The stump in the photo on the left lost its bark long ago, and its metamorphosis is at a very picturesque stage. To add more character to the scene, a combination bronze sundial and birdbath has been placed on top of the stump.

Sculptures add distinction and elegance to any microscene, often giving the setting a focal point and thereby defining the boundaries of the scene. The choice of sculptural style, whether modern, ancient or whatever, doesn't matter as long as it is tasteful and well done.

The earthy and intriguing stone on the walls is called "Driftwood" and is found in the western desert areas near extinct volcanoes. Actually, it is marble that was tossed out of an exploding volcano. If you chip away the burnt exterior, you'll find pure white marble inside.

The plants (from top left) are a Day Lily not yet in bloom; (below it) three ornamental grasses: Fiber Optic Grass, Blue Fescue and Mondo Grass; (to the stump's right) a New Guinea hybrid Impatiens, just beginning a bloom cycle; (in front of the Impatiens) Wood Sorrel, *Oxalis purpurea* (zones 8 through 10); and the yellow flowers are Strawflowers.

A freshly-cut eucalyptus branch has been left in the midst of the plants. It will have a more natural look when it dries and bleaches from the sun. In about a year, it will look like driftwood.

When you have your trees trimmed, watch for unusual pieces of branches that are being removed. The more twisted or contorted the better. "Y"-shaped, curved sections or straight pieces where other limbs have been partly cut off, all work well as attractive driftwood when aged.

Driftwood Does Not Grow On The Beach

I'll never forget a comment I overheard a lady make on seeing a piece of driftwood in a flower bed, *"Why did they put that piece of driftwood there? We are not within 500 miles of the ocean."*

This lady obviously had never been in a forest or near a stream coming from a forest. Downed trees and branches in forests get washed into streams by heavy rain. Eventually the water in those streams reaches the ocean, but the tree parts are "drift" wood as soon as they hit the stream.

If you live close to an ocean, river or stream, you'll find driftwood, usually free for the taking. If not, a trip into rural areas or forests may be in order. Some nationally-owned forests and state forests are open to removal of small amounts of downed wood or driftwood if you get a permit from the ranger station. They will usually issue the permit on the spot at no charge.

The stump in the photo at the top of this page was found washed up on a sandbar of a stream. The roots were trimmed to make a natural pot stand for the patio.

On your left is a scene where a stump is used as a sculpture stand with a contorted branch of driftwood as a complement. A bough of Bougainvillea spreads languorously beside the original cast aluminum sculpture, entitled, "Welcome."

Below is a Saguaro Cactus stump found in a Sedona, Arizona furniture store that was having a going-out-of-business sale. It was part of their window decoration. With a little cutting, drilling and staining, I made it into a base for my globe. It seemed fitting for the sometimes twisted-up world that we live in. It is normally used indoors.

Driftwood Dresses Up Bland Spots

Driftwood can be used to add appeal to what might be a rather bland spot in your landscape. In the photo on your left, a large contorted piece adds a natural look to the area and covers a hard-to-plant section.

A Handy And Decorative Herb Garden

If you have a large garden, often the spot where you grow herbs and vegetables is a distance from the kitchen. The photo below illustrates how you can have your most used herbs close-by in a Mexican pocket pot.

In this case, the pot is serving two purposes. It is located close to the kitchen for easy access to the cook. And second, a microscene has been created using the pot as a focal point.

Pocket pots also look fabulous when filled with strawberry plants—even after the strawberries have been picked.

Branches And Logs Make Great Terraces

Or Planters

Very often people will put up with a messy, dirty unattractive tree just because it is on their property. If you plan to keep the home for a few years, you might improve the value by cutting down the ugly tree and putting in a nice ornamental one. There are several trees in each zone that grow very fast.

The branches and logs from cut down trees make great natural planters or planting terraces for embankments and hillsides.

The photo shows some logs being used as terraces. The most interesting part of the log was put at the end of the terrace for visual impact. A miniature gladiola bulb lost in planting is coming up between branch cutoffs.

An Ivy Geranium with a few blooms is cascading from behind the railroad tie above. Meanwhile, one of the most fabulous new blooming plants is on the left. It is called Blue Wonder, *Scaevola aemula* (zones 8 through 10), and blooms continuously from spring until first frost.

Eucalyptus trees grow prolifically but have very weak branches. A fierce windstorm broke three main branches which were put to good use in terracing the steep embankment shown in the top photo.

Steps were notched into the rocky bank and one half inch steel rebar was driven in along the edge of the steps. Rebar is an inexpensive concrete reinforcing rod available at brickyards and building supply houses. Plumbing pipe could also be used but doesn't blend in as well. After the rebar was set, the logs were laid against it and fresh soil filled in behind.

As you probably see, all the logs are not straight, but that will make the scene more natural-looking when it grows in.

Ivy Geraniums, Asparagus Ferns and Bermuda Buttercups were planted. After four months, the bottom photo shows that it has zestfully filled in with parts of some logs still showing. In another three months, the steep rocky embankment, once thought unplantable will become vibrantly beautiful.

Don't worry about the logs rotting and the plants tumbling down. It usually takes from five to fifteen years for most logs to completely rot away. By that time the plants will be so firmly established that it won't make any difference. If you are still concerned, coat the soil sides of the logs with creosote or plastic tar, available in most hardware stores.

Garden Ornaments Are Design Tools

Garden ornaments, sculptures, statues and structures are important tools for making a garden more interesting, as long as they are used in microscenes. Used randomly, they will have little effect.

The deer shown on your left took about two hours to make from a downed tree with a chain saw, drill and electric screw driver. By leaving the bark on the tree, it will continue to look authentic as it ages. Pick a spot with foliage that partially obscures it for the best effect.

The white flowering bush in front of it is a Firethorn bush, *Pyracantha fortuneana* (zones 6 through 10, although some varieties are hardy in zone 5). These flowers turn into green berries which turn red in winter and stay on until spring—that is, if the birds don't pick them. Many small birds like this bush for building nests because cats and other animals can't get by the sharp thorns that form inside behind the foliage.

Firethorn bushes can be pruned to form interesting shapes—even rough topiaries—which can be maintained at about the same size. However, if left unpruned, they can grow to about 15 feet high in 10 years. The flowers in spring and red berries in the winter make this a colorful addition to any garden.

Shed Conventional Thinking To Create Scenes

Often you can create charming little scenes by shedding conventional thinking. Before throwing anything away that is large, rusted or worn out, think of whether it might make a interesting garden ornament.

There are a few criteria for using unconventional items. Could plants grow in it? Could I make it look like it was discarded and just landed accidentally in a spot? If I spray painted it in an unusual color, would that add to its appeal?

In the photo, the elaborate top of this birdbath looks as if it was thrown away and came to land there. Actually, that is almost true. After a windstorm blew the birdbath, over breaking its base, the choices were to try to buy a base (they usually come in sets) or discard it.

Then the thought occurred to me that it might look good just sitting on the ground. I tried several spots, but the edge of this dry gravel stream looked the most interesting and became its permanent home.

A piece of English Ivy was pulled over it from a nearby patch and a piece of driftwood dropped on the edge of the stream to make the scene more natural.

A prostrate juniper bush shades its back with a bunch of Fountain Grass by its side. In the foreground is a gardenia. Sprinklers keep it full of water, and birds still frolic in the bath in the summer time.

Don't Discard Worn Out Wheelbarrows!

If fact, if you know anyone in the construction industry, ask them to keep their eyes open for discarded wheels barrows. Usually, construction crews will wear out one or more a year.

Why are they so important? Well, for one thing, they make wonderful flower beds; and being mobile, they can be easily wheeled around until you find just the right spot. The older they are, the better garden ornaments they make. Actually, they make a microscene all by themselves.

Though hardly recognizable from this angle, there is a wheelbarrow under those flowers in the photo. Mixed colors of trailing *Lobelia erinus* (zones 3 through 10), planted from seeds overflows its sides while a sentinel yellow Coreopsis keeps watch.

This photo was shot right at dusk, when colors are the most vibrant and saturated, to show you the drama of this scene. Safflower blades rise from the grass in front and a corner of a large Bronze Fountain Grass bush, *Pennisetum setaceum* (zones 4 through 10), appears on the right.

Rural antique shows are often good sources of great items you can use as garden ornaments. Of course, they have to be reasonably priced because they will eventually deteriorate from weathering. That is, unless you plan on painting them. If so, use a two-part epoxy resin instead of conventional paints. The epoxy will make them last a very long time, especially if you coat any part touching the ground.

You Should Not Miss!

Sunlight, at various times of day, has an amazing effect on the appearance of a garden. A bright midday sun washes out the brilliance of colors. Green tones appear to run together with no definition.

However, for an hour just after dawn and the hour before sunset, the depth and saturation of colors is magnificent. Flowers and foliage are almost as dazzling as gemstones. Photographers and artists call those two periods "magic hours".

For the most exquisite visual pleasure you'll ever experience (if you have a beautiful place), try to be in your garden at least one of those hours each day during the growing season.

Artists, photographers and sensitive garden designers like myself find that we enjoy a special, unusual but enchanting feeling during this unique time. If you've never experienced those hours in a beautiful place, try it. That alone is worth a hundred times the price of this book!

Many of the photos in this book were taken during the magic hours for the selfish pleasure of all of us. The photo on the left was shot at the beginning of a sunset magic hour. Notice how rich the wood looks, and how deep and full the other colors are.

Whimsey Is Very Appropriate!

Gardens are happy places. Why not add a little whimsey to encourage more happiness? Time and a little thought can make a rather mundane object like a grape arbor come alive whimsically as shown in the photo.

I carved the figure from a 2x12 redwood board with a jigsaw in a little over an hour. Sanding, finishing and mounting took three hours—a Saturday project.

The sister to the grape arbor man was also carved from redwood, bleached for a different look, varnished and mounted in front of a tough-to-plant embankment.

Cedar, cypress and redwood are the best woods to use outdoors because they deteriorate very slowly. Redwood bleaches naturally in the sun to a lustrous silvergrey. If you apply a clear finish, it will maintain its rich red color. Cedar and cypress sometimes weather to a grey, but also they can turn black, depending on the location. However, if you like their original color, it can be preserved by finishing with a "boat" spar varnish.

Don't use spar varnish from a hardware or paint store. They don't stand up well to ultraviolet rays, no matter what the store salesperson tells you. Get a boat spar varnish from a boat supply store. The grape arbor man and his sister have been outside for 10 years and were refinished only once two years ago.

Now there is an even better product that you won't have to redo for 20 years. It's a new clear polyester casting resin that doesn't yellow in sunlight, available in plastic supply stores. You can brush on a sealer and then a finish coat of this resin, and forget painting after that.

In the photo, the embankment was terraced with driftwood logs and planted with hardy Ivy Geraniums in three colors, three colors of Lantana, and white Alyssum.

In this scene, each element complements and relates to the other elements. The dried reed fence covering provides a warm contrast to the coolness of the dry stream made of gravel and black La Paz pebbles. The green bamboo is compatible with the reed. Granite boulders appear randomly in the stream as Sword Fern lines the rear bank.

Mondo Grass, *Ophiopogon* (zones 7 through 10), forms clumpy islands with a Maidenhair tree growing from its mossy (Baby Tears) bank. And what better symbol could be found than this freestyle concrete fish statue? The Oriental-style redwood light symbolizes a house on the bank of the stream.

Although this scene was carefully planned, the randomness of the plant placement makes it look like the only contributions by man were the fence and statue. The effect is that it almost tells a story—or one could be easily created to fit this scene.

The Maidenhair Tree, *Gingko biloba* (zones 4 through 10), makes an exotic shade tree that often lives for over a hundred years. In the fall its leaves turn to a golden yellow, making it one of most handsome deciduous trees.

The Maidenhair is one of the oldest trees on earth. Leaf fossils have been found that date back before the last Ice Age. Obviously very hardy, this tree was one of the first signs of plant life to sprout near ground zero in Hiroshima, Japan, where the atomic bomb was dropped.

Follies Are Fun And Add Interest

If you want people to be in awe of your garden rather than saying, *"my, you have some pretty flowers,"* then you will need to give as much attention to the sculptures, statues and structures you add as you do the plants. Also, a "folly" or two will be helpful.

A folly is a reduced or enlarged sized version of some real item or structure. Follies became popular originally in England where gardening is one of the most popular national pastimes. Often you see Holland-style windmills (which are still sold in this country), or miniature London Towers. In Italy, small Leaning Towers Of Pisa are popular.

Windmills are somewhat cliche, but wishing wells never loose their charm. If you are ambitious and handy with tools, a miniature Hansel and Gretel house or a whimsical, short trolley car make adorable additions.

I created the sundial by laminating 3/8-inch redwood bender boards in a simple fixture. Although the overall creation time was only about 16 hours, it took nearly a month to finish because each lamination had to cure overnight before the next one could be added.

The plants shown in the photo are Periwinkle in the foreground, yellow Tickseed, *Coreopsis verticillata,* in the lower right, and Bronze Fountain Grass to the right with a Day Lily below the grass.

A Surprise Ground Cover

The sandy soil on this slope wouldn't support three different ground covers even though the soil was extensively amended after each attempt. You may find the ground cover that did work to be a little surprising. It is the common house plant known as the Spider Plant, *Chlorophytum comosum* (zones 8 through 10).

It is hardy, grows prolifically and even stores up water for droughts in root nodules. After it fills in the area you have chosen, the new shoots should be cut off once or twice a year. They make the cover too thick, preventing sufficient light from reaching the bottom plants. Spider Plants grow well in sun or shade, and obviously can handle the worst type of soils.

The small trees shown in the photo are Rubber Trees which were planted in double-size holes with a substantial amount of good potting soil. The original bronze sculpture is entitled, "The Graduate". I thought it was symbolic of this problem spot which is now appealing.

A Black Thumb May Be Due To Problem Soils

Frequently, I hear people say that they just can't seem to get anything to grow well in their garden. Often it is because of the wrong choice of plants for the zone, putting sun plants in the shade, or shade plants in the sun, too little or too much water, or lack of fertilization.

Many plants grow poorly in soils not suited to their needs. If you are having a problem, dig a six-inch diameter hole straight down about a foot and take the soil to your local nursery. A good horticulturist can visually determine soil inadequacies and recommend a soil amendment to correct the problem.

The shaded area in the photo had a pecular condition. Two ground covers, Asparagus Ferns, *Asparagus rumosus* (zones 9 and 10), and Creeping Red Fescue were doing well, yet a variety of shade-type flowering plants failed to flourish. I suspected that there were some mineral salts in the sandy soil that were causing the problem.

If you live within 200 miles of salt water, often construction sand is brought in from the beaches. It is not unusual during the construction of a house for some sand to be left behind. It contains salt, and apparently that is what I had here.

Therefore, I chose the hardiest, most attractive shade plant I could find that I knew could handle some salt—the Bear's Breech, *Acanthus mollis* (zones 6 to 10). You can see the results in the photo. One warning, though. Once planted, you'll never get rid of Bear's Breech. It has tuberous roots. If you dig it up and leave behind just a tiny quarter-inch piece, another plant will come up there.

If you have a friend with a black thumb, give them a piece of the root. It will probably grow fabulously for them. (The original concrete sculpture is entitled, "Marriage.")

If you have a spot of land where nothing grows well, you can always put a structure there that might be even more inviting than plants. The gazebo stands on a spot where not even tough English Ivy would grow.

A retaining wall was built and the gazebo cantilevered out for added height to capture an extensive view of the ocean. Bougainvillea loves open trellis-type roofs and grew quickly to produce added shade. The light lavender flowers are Lily-of-the-Nile and the small purple ones are Lantana.

Nile lilies, *Agapanthus orientalis* (zones 7 to 10), are native to Egypt. The inset photo shows how spectacular they are when in bloom. The flowers, also available in white, last about a month and leave behind a round cluster of green seed pods. The pods are fascinating and the foliage is attractive for the entire growing season.

Interesting foliage is one of the key factors in creating a great garden. Plants that don't have good foliage, but have flowers that you prize, should be placed between plants with more pleasant leaves to distract attention from them.

There's Nothing Like A Backyard Swing!

Have you ever met a person who didn't like an old fashioned backyard swing? I suppose they exist, but for most of us, there is a certain nostalgia attached to gently swinging in a balmy summer breeze.

The style of swing that you prefer probably depends on your childhood experiences. Some like the tire hanging from a rope off a tree limb. Those brought up in a densely populated big city may prefer playground swings. Others may like the quaint structurally self-contained swings for two. And then there are those who remember the swing-for-two hanging from the tree limb.

Of course, those who like the latter do have a problem—the location of the swing is limited to finding a tree limb which will support the swing.

That was the case in the photo. The only tree that qualified was on a slope, and determination to have a swing under a shady tree won out.

There's another reason from a design standpoint. If you have a large natural garden, you need breaks in the constant flow of plants to create more visual interest.

The steps and swing provide a surprising but handsome break. To the left of the swing is a Rubber Tree. A Shasta Daisy, *Chrysanthemum maximum* (zones 4 through 10), is blooming beside the stair steps. In the lower left corner is an everblooming *Aster frikartii* (zones 5 through 10).

Any Excuse For A Bridge!

If you were practical, you would not have built a bridge over this shallow dry-rock stream, but designing a garden that is pleasing and exciting was the goal—not how cheaply one could do it. Of course, a good lawyer could argue that the bridge IS practical because it keeps your guests' shoes from being scarred by the rocks in the stream. This bridge in the photo on this page was built as a visual break in the scenery.

The railing of the bridge in the top left photo is only used by the shortest of gremlins, but it certainly makes a bland bridge more interesting and doesn't block the view of the flowers. The yellow flowers are Bermuda Buttercups, the purple to the far right is a Scented Geranium, and the red flowers on the plant in front of the center rock is a Fairy Duster, *Calliandra california* (zone 9, 10). There are several other blooming plants in this scene that are not yet in season.

The redwood bridge in the bottom left photo spans a brook that feeds the waterfall below. A small wood-block stool on a concrete pyramid block offers a quiet resting place where one can enjoy the babbling brook.

Address Maintenance Problems Creatively

Sometimes we must address maintenance problems of a garden in a practical manner such as how do we service plants without damaging those around them?

For example, the steep embankment, in the photo to your left, was terraced with railroad ties to a certain point below where the bank became too steep. Consequently, tall plants were chosen to cover up the steep area.

During the planting behind the railroad ties, it was realized that after planting the tall plants below, access to those above for weeding, pruning overgrowth, deadheading, etc., would be difficult. Some sturdy steps were needed that would be unobtrusive yet attractive.

The solution you see is an abstract sculptural stair which is visually interesting yet strong and practical. Mitered 4x4s were cemented into the ground and into the embankment. People seeing them never realize that they are stairs.

The orange flowers on the left and upper middle are Nasturtiums, the purple flowers on the top left and middle are Blue Wonder. Red gladiolas are on the lower left with a peach Canna peeking in. Red geraniums are at the top center with some white Alyssum below them. The leggy silver grey plant in the center is long-blooming Jeruseleum Sage, *Phlomis fruticosa* (zones 4 through 10), which is getting ready to cover itself with yellow flowers.

Whimsey And Playfulness Are Compatible

With Beauty

How can one be somber and serious when walking through a captivating garden? Watch people emerge from public gardens. They will usually have smiles on their faces. I find myself smiling when I walk through my garden. Natural beauty seems to make us feel happy.

The forest scenes in Greek mythology are loaded with playful, fun creatures. Many of these creatures are available as inexpensive statues. If they appeal to you, add a few to your garden setting. Those who are literate in Greek mythology will appreciate the significance. Buy the ones made from concrete or other substances that will stand up outdoors. Those made from Hydrocal or plaster will deteriorate in time.

The original bronze and stainless steel sculpture, "Dancers," in the photo to the left appear to be frolicking between the rose bush, Day Lily and Bronze Fountain Grass. Any sculpture that suggests movement in a garden has an excellent effect.

Color Of Foliage Is More Important

Than Color Of Flowers!

Many gardeners try to match just the right color of flowers with the ones nearby. That is a very tedious, time-consuming process that often yields poor visual results.

First, most flowers aren't in bloom at exactly the same time, and in many cases, the flowers will be there for only two or three weeks. The rest of the growing season, you'll be looking at foliage.

Mix the colors of foliage and you will get a much more pleasing display throughout the year. In this scene, the yellow Gazanias have blue-grey leaves, the geraniums have a yellow green and the Shasta Daisies, have a dark green. The colors don't clash and the scene is visually interesting without flowers. You'll be seeing many more examples of using foliage colors and textures effectively throughout this book.

The Easter Island gods certainly inspired the original patinated bronze sculpture, "Diamond Head," set in this meadow. A luxuriant Jade Tree poses above the sculpture.

Plants In Pots In A Natural Garden?

To some it may seem incongruous to put plants in pots in a natural garden However, they fall into the same category as sculptures and garden ornaments. Used sparingly, plants in interesting pots provide more visual impact and add a sophisticated appeal to your garden.

Also, you can use plants not compatible with your weather zone by keeping them inside during the winter. The Cymbidium Orchids shown in the bottom left photo are an excellent example.

The top left photo displays a stately full grown Pampas Grass, *Cortaderia selloana* (zones 6 to 10), behind the original stainless steel sculpture, "Heredity." Pampas normally grows to six feet in diameter and eight feet in height, so leave plenty of space. They look well when placed in the corner of a lot.

The Pampas Grass in the photo on this page is showing off its fluffy fall plumes. This plant is too large to bring inside, but is smaller than a normal Pampas because the pot restricts its growth, similar to potted bonsai trees that are kept small by using diminutive pots.

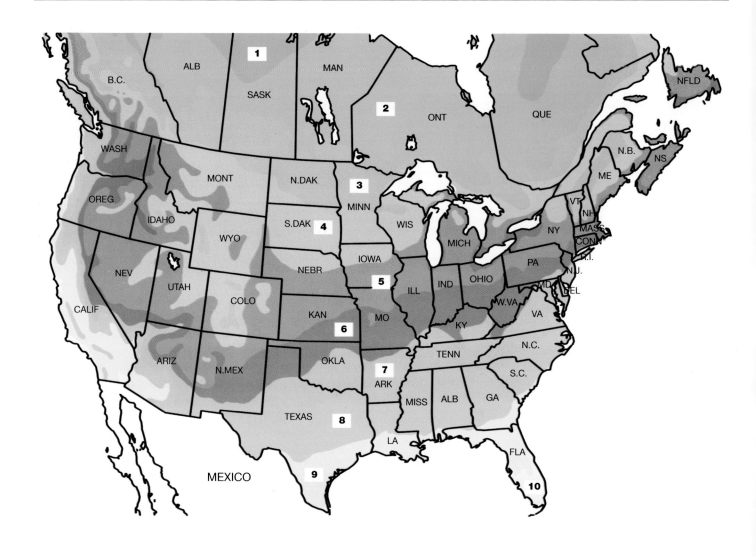

Range of Average Annual Minimum Temperatures For Each Zone

Zone 1	Below -50°F	Zone 6	-10° to 0°
Zone 2	-50 to -40°	Zone 7	0° to 10°
Zone 3	-40 to -30°	Zone 8	10° to 20°
Zone 4	-30 to -20°	Zone 9	20° to 30°
Zone 5	-20 to -10°	Zone 10	30° to 40°

Courtesy of the Agricultural Research Service, U.S. Dept. of Agriculture

The Importance Of Zones

One of the biggest chores facing a person who decides to create a unique garden is choosing the right plants. To the uninitiated it may sound like fun. Just get out the nursery catalogs or plant picture books and go wild. I must admit that if you could create a garden without limitation by just picking plants from those books, it would be awesome. However, as a practical matter, that is impossible. You are going to be restricted to plants that will grow in the climate zone where you live.

The U.S. Department of Agriculture has produced a map, shown on the opposite page, that defines roughly the various climate zones of North America. These zones delineate the most common low temperatures usually experienced. For example, Zone 5 usually doesn't have cold weather exceeding 20 degrees below 0 Fahrenheit.

Basically, a plant which has been specified for Zone 5 will not survive at temperatures less than 20 degrees below 0° F. Sometimes a prolonged period of temperatures around -20° below will kill a plant specified for Zone 5. Heavy mulch or other covering can allow a plant specified for Zone 6 (0 to -10 degrees) to survive in Zone 5.

On the other hand, there are plants that won't go into dormancy unless the temperature drops into the twenties. Some herbacious perennials won't come back in the spring unless they've had a few months of dormancy. Or if they do come back, they will be very weak and probably won't survive the next winter.

Then there are plants that require steady high temperatures to develop properly. Corn and melons especially fall into this category.

You may look at the zone map and see that you are in Zone 9 or 10 and say, *"Wow! I can grow anything where I live."* Not true. Some parts of Zone 9 and 10 are desert, and many plants require high humidity. Areas of Zone 10 are kept cool by ocean breezes and never get above 80 degrees. Plants that require high temperatures won't do well there, nor will those that need a freeze to go into dormancy.

That's just the basics of zones. The subject is much more involved and technical and shouldn't concern you if you stick to plants specifically oriented to your zone. That is the danger of ordering from mail-order plant catalogs. If the catalog does not give the zonal range for a plant, don't order it until you know what the range is. In my opinion, any nursery catalog that does not give the zones for their plants is not very reputable.

Early in my gardening career, I wasted literally hundreds of dollars buying plants out of my zone even though I knew the implications of the zones. I figured that if it was only one zone away, it would grow for me. Wrong!

Local nurseries are your best source. Of course, they want to sell as many plants as possible, but they also want you to come back as a regular customer. Rarely will they sell a plant that is not suited for the local zone.

Choosing plants from your zone is not total insurance that the plants will survive. This is particularly true if you live in a hilly area or near a large body of water. Hills, lakes and oceans can create microclimates that have temperatures contradictory to your zone.

We've all heard microclimatic weather terms such as "lake effect" or "banana belt." Lake effect means that a nearby lake is causing a warmer or cooler temperature than the area further away from the lake. Banana belt means an area with normally warmer temperatures than the surrounding area. You can have a small microclimate on just part of your property. A low spot, or an area along the side of your house where the wind whips through, may have lower temperatures than the rest of your property.

Perennials Or Annuals?

For a few moments, let's use both sides of our brains and bring some logic into the design of a natural garden. I assume that having a colorful garden for as many months as the weather allows is your goal.

If so, then that means having a lot of different flowers in bloom every month. If you choose annuals and have a big garden, your spring planting chores will be sizeable. Annuals, for those of you that don't know, last for only one year's growing season, unless they are self-seeding. Wildly dropped seeds growing in unpredictable places can mess up your design if you don't pull them up. Perennials usually last several years, and many go on for 10, 15, 20 years or more. Logically, annuals don't make a lot of sense due to the yearly planting labor and replacement expense.

"But", you say, "I just love 'X' annuals. I don't care if they bloom for only a couple of weeks and I have to plant them every year."

If that is the case, don't plant huge clumps of them. Put small groups of annuals between perennials. That way you won't have a big spot without color and monotonous foliage for the majority of the year—a design faux pas.

The annuals I use have to fit two of the following four criteria: one, they must bloom for more than a month or have two blooming periods during the year. Two, they should grow quickly from seed with little soil preparation. Three, if they self-seed, it must be localized and controllable. And four, they ought to bloom when most plants are not flowering.

When a garden is newly planted, many perennials as well as shrubs may take several years to reach their mature size. This is the ideal time to use annuals as filler between perennials until they mature. Also, some herbacious perennials are slow to come up in the spring. Early flowering annuals can fill in for them.

In the zone where these photos were taken, there are only a few annuals I use regularly: white and purple Alyssum, trailing Lobelia, Nasturtium and Sweet William, *Dianthus barbatus* (zones 4 through 10).

On the previous page, the white flowers in the top half of the photo are Alyssum. They are being used as filler until the permanent plants are available at the local nursery. Alyssum blooms up to six months in the cooler zones and practically year-round in zones 9 and 10. They are self-seeding, but usually fairly localized.

Trailing Lobelia also blooms for up to six months and doesn't self-seed very readily. The mixed color seed combinations are most attractive. The wheel barrow on page 25 has Lobelia planted in it.

Nasturtiums flower very early in spring and provide color in areas that are slow to come up. Their vivid red, yellow and orange blossoms are around for a few months, but I usually cut them back or pull them up as the other flowers come into their prime. Nasturtium seeds are large and usually don't travel too far.

Choose The Longest Blooming Perennials

For Key Spots

Think for a moment about which spots in your garden will be seen the most often, or which spot comes into view first. Obviously, one flower in each key microscene should always have its best dress on. There are not many perennials that bloom all season long, but there are a few. Whatever ones are available in your zone should be used in those keynote spots with those that have shorter flower cycles.

In the bottom photo on your left is a Tickseed. This simple yellow flower is dependable and hardy and almost always in bloom from spring until fall. Like most flowers, they need to be deadheaded (spent flowers removed) regularly to keep them looking fresh.

Don't leave spent flowers on any plant until they go to seed. First, they are ugly; and second, by removing the spent flower when it wilts, the plant will produce more blossoms. Think of a flowering plant as a mother hen. She's trying desperately to make babies. If you leave the eggs there, she'll sit on them until they hatch. If you remove the eggs, she'll keep laying more.

Ivy Geraniums, *Pelagonium peltatum* (perennial zones 8 to 10, annuals elsewhere), are delightful, very long blooming— six to twelve months depending on the zone—and are available in five colors. They are perfect for hillsides and slopes, but work well in flat areas, too.

In the top photo, an errant Nasturtium seed was allowed to grow down the middle between red and lavender Geraniums. The original iron and bronze gong announces the entrance of a Japanese-style guest house.

Day Lilies And A Special Iris Are High

On The List

Day Lilies, *Hemerocallis* (zones 4 to 10), with their long thin blade-like leaves, make an impressive contrast with other perennials in microscenes. They bloom on and off from spring until frost—almost year-around in moderate climate zones. In six months, you may have six waves of blooming periods that last two weeks each. There are literally dozens of colors, and most deadhead themselves. Day Lilies grow from bulbs and need to be divided every three to five years, so you'll have more to use or give to friends.

One of the most dramatic perennials is shown on the left. Some people call it the Butterfly Plant because when it is in bloom, from a distance the flowers look like a swarm of butterflies. Actually, you can see in the photo at the bottom of the page that the flower looks like a cross between an iris and an orchid. It is also known as the African Iris or Fortnight Lily.

This unusual iris, *Dietes Iridoides* (zones 8 through 10), requires a little more maintenance than other irises because it also produces seeds. You can see the green pods in the photo. They should be removed after each two-week flowering wave.

In the photo to the top left is a Bermuda Buttercup, *Oxalis cernua* (zones 8 through 10), which is a rather spectacular yellow perennial that blooms in the late winter through spring in moderate climates. The best place to plant it is among perennials that come up mid-to-late spring or in any area that is dull or brown in winter. The lively buttercup-shaped blossoms and lush green foliage will brighten up any garden.

Some people consider them pests, as they spread rapidly by seeds and multiplying bulbs, but considering that there isn't much blooming when they are around, they are a colorful asset. These buttercups are so vigorous that thinning is necessary sometimes. But they pull out of the ground with little effort. In spring, they should be removed when other plants start to revive or when their leaves start yellowing.

Aster frikartii, the lavender flower in the bottom left photo is another long-blooming plant and an asset to any garden. This sun-loving perennial blooms constantly from spring to fall and even longer in moderate climates. Its stalks are not too sturdy, so give it room to spill over the surrounding area.

To the left of the Aster is another blossom-happy plant, Scented Geranium (zones 9 and 10). This upright geranium is one of a dozen different flower foliage combinations produced by the variety. Some of them are two-tone.

The lonely, single yellow flower in the right foreground is either a late or early Day Lily, because the plant finished its bloom cycle a week prior.

Long Stemmed Roses Create Design Concerns

Rose bushes and climbers are easy to fit into a garden design, but because long-stemmed roses have such scrawny stalks and sparse foliage, their location must be chosen carefully.

Public rose gardens are so unsightly that they almost turn a good designer's stomach. The reason is that gardeners for those facilities choose a plot of ground and plant row after row of long-stemmed roses. The result looks like a briar patch with pretty flowers on top.

The best place to locate these roses is against a low contrast wall as shown in the photo. The stalks and sparse leaves are much less noticeable, and your eyes are drawn to the flowers. Make sure overhead sprinklers don't wet the blooms. Water literally destroys rose petals. Buried soaker hose or shrub-type base sprinklers are best.

Tall In The Shade

The dullness of this wood column which supports a cantilevered roof is broken up by this sprite Fuchsia, *Fuchsia hybrida* (zones 9 and 10). The ballerina-skirted blossoms appear intermittently during the growing season. The plant has been staked to keep it in front of the post and out of the path beside it. It will sprawl normally and looks good under trees where there's little or very short ground cover.

If you are excited and ready to get started designing and planting a new garden, you'll get a big surprise when you go to the nursery with a big shopping list of plants. Very few of what you want will be available. Nurseries only stock flowers when they are in bloom with the exception of bulbs and roses. Sometimes you can order them immediately before or after the blooming period, but more likely not.

Of course, that means you must plan where each plant will go and leave spots empty until the plants you need become available. If you start in spring, September may come before you've filled in all the blanks.

Be aware that not all nurseries carry a full line of every plant for your zone. Therefore, it is wise to visit or call all of them regularly if you know which plants you need. Be careful who you talk to, especially at big nurseries, because many of the employees only have a smattering of knowledge useful to you.

Flashy Plants Need Color-Corrected Locations

The Eulalia Grass, *Miscanthus sinensis "Variegatus"* (zones 9 to 10), in the photo is an incredibly striking plant, but in this location, its foliage is simply too dramatic. Every time a person looks in the general direction, their eyes are immediately drawn to this plant.

The reason is that the contrast between the plant and the background is too strong. The plant was moved to a spot next to a swimming pool surrounded by grey flagstone and granite boulders. This reduced the contrast considerably so it doesn't jump out visually, yet the plant is still inviting.

Add A Fourth Dimension To Your Garden

Many varieties of flowers have an aroma, but usually only if you get your nose close to the flower. However, there are a few that permeate the air around them with delightful scents. The most common one that flourishes in many zones is Honeysuckle, *Lonicera* (zones 4 through 10), shown in the bottom photo. Some varieties have little aroma. Night Blooming Jasmine, *Cestrum nocturnum*, is one of the kings of perfumery, but it will grow only in the southerly zones, nine and ten.

For the best effect, locate any aromatic plant next to a walkway or path where a person must nearly brush against the plant as they walk by. The scent is so pleasing that most people will linger to enjoy it more.

From a design standpoint, vines such as Honeysuckle and Jasmine can be used to break up the monotony of a fence or wall.

Control Vines To Maintain The Visual Impact

Some vines grow slowly while others are aggressive fast growers like the English Ivy, *Hedera helix* (zones 4 through 10), shown in the top photo. Whatever type you have, you must keep an eye on it. If you let it cover the entire wall or fence, you have lost an interesting design tool. Keep it thinned out so that the structure shows through as shown by both photos. Don't let the ivy crawl on the ground into other areas, because it will put down roots and it is difficult to destroy.

In the top photo, the original concrete sculpture, "Delta Cee" is shown.

Bamboo—A Visual Pleasure If Controlled

Bamboo can be an excellent designer's tool. If silhouetted against a contrasting background as shown in the photo, the outline of the branches and leaves contributes an exotic feeling and unusual visual interest.

One or two plants should be used in microscenes for the best effect. Stands of bamboo can be used as wind breaks or to block your neighbor's view of your yard as it often grows to a height of 12 feet and sometimes higher depending on the variety.

There are two types of bamboo, running or clumping. Unfortunately, running bamboo is one of the most invasive plants. Each spring it sends out fibrous runners which will travel under sidewalks—even shallow foundations. Suddenly, shoots will pop up in the most unexpected places.

There is, however, an easy way to control it. Simply plant the bamboo in a pot with no hole in the bottom. Bury the pot with the top edge about two inches higher than the ground surface. In the spring, check the plants occasionally to see if any runners have climbed out of the pot and clip them off.

With most varieties of bamboo, you have to harvest last years growth after the new shoots have reached six feet in height or more. The old growth turns yellow and most of the leaves will fall off.

Cut down the old stalks to the ground, trim the branches off, and you'll have some great sticks for staking plants or making kids' fishing poles.

Remember when you buy bamboo to ask if it is the running or clumping type so you will know what to expect.

Unusual Trees For A Captivating Landscape

Trees with unusual shapes and colors planted in mixed contrast with each other create an appealing look that you won't get tired of viewing.

The Honey Locust, *Gleditsia triacanthus* (zones 5 to 10), shown in the photo is a deciduous tree (loses its leaves in the winter) that begins spring with yellow foliage resembling a flock of yellow birds. A month later the leaves will change to a mint green color.

By having different leaf colors and textures grouped together, each tree stands out showing its individual character. In the upper left is the branch of a Blue Acacia, and behind the Honey Locust is a dark green, twisting Hollywood Juniper. On its right is a Blue Atlas Cedar, and to the far right is a medium green oak.

If you don't have a book that shows the trees available in your zone, get catalogs from the major mail-order nurseries (listed on page 177). These dream catalogs have a very broad selection of the most interesting trees within each zone range.

Don't order from the catalogs unless you want a two to four-foot tree. Just use the catalogs to arm yourself with the knowledge of which trees you like, their mature size and survival zones. Then go to your local nursery and have them order a bigger tree for you.

The top photo shows a Hollywood Juniper, *Juniperus chinensis torulosa* (zones 5 through 10), in more detail. This tree's twisted nature (hence the name "Hollywood") is due to the tips of the branches seeking a clear view of the sun and trying to avoid the shadows of other branches or anything that blocks its view. No matter where they are planted, these trees go through the same contortions.

Junipers are among the hardiest of trees, are pest and drought resistant and grow in almost any soil except clays and marshes. There are numerous varieties of junipers in an array of shapes and sizes, from those that grow horizontally to the ground, to tall stately giants.

One of the best books on trees is *Stirling Macoboy's What Tree Is That?* It is loaded with color photographs and details about each tree, but it is out-of-print. You might find it in your local library.

The blue Atlas Cedar in the photo, *Cedrus atlantica glauca* (zones 6 to 10), not only has a unique color, but develops a shape relative to its environment. In this location, it gets direct sun only for the last couple hours of the day. Without any pruning or tieing, it has espaliered itself to the wall of the house. Its colorful shape will add fascination to any garden.

When given full sun, it achieves a little more symmetry but still has an impetuous abstract form as you can see in the photo on the previous page. I have managed to bonsai one that is now 18 years old and only 28 inches tall from the bottom of its pot. However, it has required twice as much training and attention as other bonsai trees. That shows an independence for shape much stronger than other trees.

The Atlas Cedar grows in most soils that have good drainage. but it is not drought resistant until it is at least seven or eight years old.

Stately Trees

One of the most elegant evergreen trees is the Norfolk Island Pine, *Araucaria heterophylla* (zones 9 and 10). I'm not sure why it is not seen more often, because it is relatively pest free and drought resistant once established. It has a very symmetrical shape when it is young as you can see in the top quarter of the tree, but as it gets older, the lower branches drape in a relaxed ski jump profile.

Don't place it too close to an old established tree, because this causes a nutritional deficiency even with regular fertilization. And be careful not to overfertilize. The results often include the loss of symmetry, overproduction of branches and needles, and a contorted trunk.

The Norfolk Island Pine is adaptable to many soils as long as there is good drainage, but prefers a sandy content.

Another distinctive evergreen is the *Podocarpus gracilor* (zones 8 through 10), more commonly called the Fern Pine. The cute, little yellow umbrellas are new shoots that appear briefly on the tips of the branches of established trees in the spring. Within a few weeks, they turn green matching the other thin-fluted leaves.

The foliage is so dense that you can train these trees into interesting shapes by pruning. Even though the branches start at the ground, they can be pruned away to create a shade tree as shown by the one directly behind.

Or, you can prune and maintain this tree in a perfectly conical shape. In a natural garden, it looks best if the shape is a little unruly and asymmetrical.

There are several varieties of the *Podocarpus* family with different shapes, mature sizes and leaf sizes. One variety sprawls like a willow and has much finer sized leaves than the one in the photo. It looks good along side of a stream, pond or pool.

In the realm of flowering trees, the Blue Acacia, *Acacia Baileyana* (zones 6 through 10), is one of the most beautiful all year long. Chains of yellow blossoms appear for about one month in spring. During the rest of the year this evergreen tree is a magnificent powder blue. When the tree is flowering, florists use cut branches from it in arrangements and call it "Golden Mimosa."

The Blue Acacia is a native of Australia and one of the fastest growing trees. Starting with a five-gallon size, it can reach the dimensions shown in the photo (15x15 feet) in three to five years.

It requires regular pruning to attain the shape that you desire—especially when very young. This acacia develops long gangly top branches during the first few years which should be pruned back to make it grow fuller. Any branch that gets disproportionately long should be pruned back. This encourages more branching and results in a fuller shape.

The Blue Acacia grows well in many soils but prefers sandy well-drained types. Do not plant in marshy areas or over water, because that will kill it quickly.

Fertilizing lightly every three months during its formative years, will cause fast growth and development. However, you may have to prune twice a year, if you choose this treatment.

t>22

Having Fruit Trees Without The Pests

Many people choose fruit trees because they like the spring flowers and the fruit bonus. The Purple Plum in the photo has the most exquisite deep maroon foliage and dainty white flowers in the spring. This is a favorite for natural gardens because its color makes a nice mix with other trees and plants.

However, like all fruit trees, the fruit attracts a lot of pests, especially aphids, which damage other plants. It is difficult to eradicate most pests without using pesticides. Those who choose not to have fruit trees have considerably fewer pest problems.

There is an alternative if you like the foliage and flowers of certain fruit trees and are willing to forego the fruit. You can avoid the pest problems by cutting off the flowering tips of the branches after the flowers are spent.

You can also control the height of trees by pruning. The Purple Plum normally achieves a mature height of 15 feet. This one has been severely pruned back after flowering every year because I want to keep it short so as to not block the view. After 10 years, it is only about eight feet tall. It was ready to be pruned when this photo was taken.

A Variety Of Plants Creates Biological Balance

There is a significant advantage to having a wide variety of plants on your landscape because specific insects are attracted to particular plants. The more insects you have, the more predator insects will come. Predator insects often destroy many of the pests that damage plants. In my botanical garden, with over 800 plants including trees, shrubs, flowers and ground covers, the pest infestation in the last 10 years has been so minimal that I find it hard to remember the last occurrence.

Japanese Black Pine—The Designer's Dream Tree

A bonsai-styled Japanese Black Pine is by far the most interesting tree for use in natural microscenes because of its flowing sculptural appearance. Under the tree, rounded stream pebbles, large stones, boulders and clumps of decorative grasses work best in creating an overall design as shown by the photo.

Of course, if you have a brook, pond or natural looking pool, a bonsai pine overhanging it would be an appealing touch. The green grass in the photo is Mondo Grass. The blue grass is Blue Fescue, *Festuca ovina glauca* (zones 4 through 10). Be sure to add a piece or two of driftwood to the scene.

Japanese Black Pines, *Pinus Thunbergiana* (zones 5 through 10), don't grow naturally in the shape you see in the photo. They grow fairly straight up in much the same shape as most pines. This tree was pruned and shaped to make it look this way.

In a nursery, a bonsai-styled tree like this one would sell for about $500. I paid only $50 for it as a common nursery tree. Originally, the tree was six feet high, but I spent an hour pruning, bending and wiring it into the bonsai style. That made it about a foot shorter. The styling is what gives it a high value because very few people know how to do this fairly simple conversion.

Within a year after it was transplanted, it filled out and looked similar to its appearance today. Black Pines are very slow growing trees. The tree in the photo is about 15 years old. In the following pages, I'll show you how to create one for yourself.

A.

B.

C.

How To Turn A $50 Tree Into A $500 Tree

In One Hour!

The only tools you will need are wire cutters, for soft aluminum or copper wire, and pruning pliers. If your local nursery doesn't have any Japanese Black Pines in stock, don't order one because you may not get a good specimen. Any Black Pine can be bonsai styled, but some are easier to modify and look better when finished. Therefore, you will want to pick the best one from a quantity of trees.

You may have to call several nurseries before you find one with plentiful stock. If there is a Japanese community in your city, nurseries serving them will be the best source.

A tree that is five to six feet tall from the bottom of its pot is the best size to style. After you have read the following instructions, you will have a good idea of which tree to pick at the nursery. Although I'm demonstrating this technique with a fairly straight tree, many of those with contorted trunks can be made into unique and attractive bonsai-styled trees.

A front view of the tree is shown in Photo A on the opposing page. Photo B is a side view. You will notice that it has very few branches facing to the back, and its trunk is curved.

This tree was chosen because the curving trunk makes it easier to create a slanted wind-blown look—one of the most desired bonsai styles. The lack of branches in the rear will be changed by bending side branches toward the back. Black Pines have rubbery branches that are easy to bend without breaking. In fact, that is a necessary characteristic of any tree that you want to convert to a bonsai style.

Photo C shows the angle in which I plan to plant this tree. The planting angle dictates how the tree will be styled.

D.

E.

F.

G.

Disguising The Symmetry

The branches of Black Pines radiate in groups of three to six from three or four nodes, usually without any branches in between the nodes on a six foot tree. Photo D shows the bottom branches which radiate from one junction. One of the principles of bonsai-styling is to disguise the radial branch symmetry. You will see how to do this in the following pages.

Photo E shows the second level of branches from the bottom up. Most bonsai trees are styled from the bottom up because you can shorten a branch, but you can't make it longer. Therefore, the proportionate length of the upper branches is determined by the length of the bottom branches.

Photo F shows the third level of branches. Photo G displays the fourth level and top. As I progress with each step in styling this tree, you will be able to look back at these photos to see the difference.

You may be wondering if there is a difference between a "bonsai tree" and a "bonsai-styled tree. Yes, there is. A bonsai tree is potted and is no more than 36 inches in height from the bottom of the pot to the top of the tree.

Before we go to the next step, you will need to obtain some copper or aluminum wire. You will need 12 feet of one-quarter inch diameter wire, three feet of one-eighth inch and three feet of one-sixteenth inch. Copper wire is expensive, so most bonsai artists use aluminum that has been anodized bronze or a copper color. The darker color makes it less obvious on the tree during the training period.

The odds are against your local hardware store having this wire in stock, but they may be able to order it for you. If you buy the tree at a Japanese-owned nursery, they may have the wire in stock.

H.

I.

J.

L.

K.

Wiring

Before you begin to wire the tree, prop it at the angle in which it will be planted. Study each node of the branches, bending and holding them in their future position, remembering at each level what your plan for the previous level was. After you have developed a plan for each branch on the tree, then you can start wiring the bottom ones.

The largest diameter wire is used to shape the major branches. One end of it is wrapped around the trunk to anchor it, as shown in Photo H. Then the wire is wrapped around the branch to the end.

Photo I shows the bottom level of branches after they have been wired. The one-eighth inch wire is used for shaping the medium-size branches growing from each main branch as you can see in this photo.

The small diameter wire is used on the smallest branches. Each piece of wire must be anchored to the branch larger than the one you are shaping, otherwise the wire will not hold the shape you are trying to achieve.

Photo J shows the second level of branches from the bottom of the tree. You will notice that only three of the branches at this node have been wired. This is because bonsai artists have found over centuries of practice that Black Pines can be shaped more attractively with only three branches at each node. In the following pages, you will see how I choose which branches to eliminate.

Photo K shows the third level branches with their wires in position. Photo L shows the fourth level. The top is not going to be wired in this case, so it is not shown.

When wiring a main branch, shape all the small branches on it so that they are level with the ground. In other words, each branch should have a flat look when the wiring is completed.

M.

N.

O.

P.

It's springtime as I'm styling this tree. In the spring, Black Pines develop new shoots, commonly referred to as "candles." If you look back at the photos on page 92, you will see the candles sticking up from the branches.

Each year you will have to cut off the candles—usually during July after they have achieved their full growth for the year. Of course, if you wait until July, you will be looking at a tree full of candles for a couple of months. The candles detract from the beauty of the tree. I cut the candles in May, however they will continue to grow. I have to cut them again in July, but in the meantime, I've had a better looking tree.

Photo L shows the bottom level of branches after they have been pruned. To prune, you grasp a cone of needles at their base between your thumb and first two fingers. Whatever sticks out above your fingers is sheared off like a crew cut. There's one exception. If you want a branch to grow longer, wire the candle on the end so it points straight out, and don't cut it off.

Photo M shows the second level of branches. The one that wasn't wired has been cut off even with the trunk. You've probably noticed that the needles have been pruned to about half their normal length. There are several effects that result from this procedure. First, shorter needles are more attractive. Second, over a few years of pruning, the tree adapts and the needles grow shorter. Third, this causes a denser growth of needles because the tree is compensating for the loss. If you look at the photo of the mature Black Pine on page 88, you will see how full the branches have become from this treatment.

Photos O and P show the third and fourth levels, respectively.

R.

S.

Shown in Photo R is a view looking down through the tree from the top. You'll see that each branch points in a slightly different direction than all the other branches. Branches that had been pointing to the side are now pointing to the back.

In Photo S, you can see we have shaped the branches on all three levels so that they are parallel to the ground. This is important for the wind-swept look that is the trademark of bonsai styling. One branch of the top has been pulled down to a parallel position with a wire tied to a lower branch.

The final styling consideration is that each branch should be slightly higher or lower than the other branches on the same level. You can do this by bending the branch upward or downward as close to the trunk as possible for about three or four inches. Then bend the remaining portion of the branch so it is level with the ground.

In the following spring or summer when you remove the candles, check the wires to see if they are digging into the tree. If so, remove them and rewire. After the second year, remove all the wires and rewire only the branches that won't stay in the planned position.

By the third or fourth year, you will have only a few wires left. A branch or two may begin pointing upward, but to correct this, just tie a weight to the branch, or tie a string to a peg anchored in the ground.

Although the tree looks sparse in Photo S, it will fill out during the growing season. By the end of the second year, it will look good and grow more beautiful every year afterwards.

Other Trees That Can Be Bonsai Styled

Practically any tree that bonsai collectors grow in small pots, can be trained in the bonsai style as a larger tree growing in the ground—especially if you like the asymmetrical look.

Some upright juniper varieties make excellent bonsai-styled trees with the exception of the Hollywood Juniper shown earlier. For a native pine, the Scotch Pine works as well as the Japanese Black Pine. The Maidenhair tree, Fern Pine, Purple Plum, Japanese Red Maples and some fine-leaf natives can be styled into interesting forms.

In the top photo, a Jade Tree, *Crassula argentea* (zones 9 to 10), shown against an appropriate reed covered fence, has been pruned in the bonsai style. Jade Trees grow very fast and require pruning twice a year, but cannot be wired like other trees because their succulent branches are too soft.

Jade Trees proliferate by fragmentation, so every piece you cut off when styling—even each leaf—can grow into another Jade Tree. Just stick a piece, no matter how small, into soil, keep it moist for a while and soon you'll have another Jade Tree. They are so hardy that they will grow in any soil, sun or total shade, indoors or out and can go without water for a couple of months if necessary.

Often, people ask if topiaries are appropriate in a natural garden. The answer is yes IF a shrub, hedge or other plant is pruned in the shape of an animal, etc. Or if a wire mesh armament is covered with vines. The answer is no if you are referring to the trees where people prune sections of the branches into little round or oval puffs in a vain attempt to imitate the bonsai style. They are too structured to look natural.

A Warning About Potted Bonsai Trees

I'm appalled by people selling bonsai trees in malls and art shows because every time I've asked, the salesperson has told me, *"You can grow these trees indoors."*

That is a gross and cruel lie! The most hardy of all trees used for bonsai, the juniper, might last a year before it dies. Other species won't live nearly as long. There are few species of trees that will grow in a house, but they are not normally used for bonsai.

I've created and grown bonsai trees for over 25 years and understand most of the idiosyncrasies of the art and and science relative to this subject.

Many people think bonsai are species and just grow that way. No, they are common nursery plants that have been pruned and trained to the shapes in which they grow.

Trees are different than the plants you grow indoors, which are tropical shade plants. First, trees need lots of fresh air because it is necessary for their transpiratory systems. They require a lots of water to operate efficiently. Most houses,with their closed recirculated, dehumidified air systems, spell the death knell to bonsai trees. They also need more light than indoor plants.

Also, bonsai must be fertilized regularly but very carefully to keep their growth to an absolute minimum. Even with proper feeding, they require pruning one to three times a year depending on the species. Along with pruning comes the wiring of the branches to keep their shape attractive. Then everyone to three years at the proper time, their soil must be removed, replaced with the proper mixture and their roots pruned. In other words, potted bonsai take knowledgeable care to keep them living and looking good.

If you bought a potted bonsai and have it indoors, there may still be time to save it. Put it outdoors in light shade and buy a book on the proper care and treatment.

Growing Plants Around Bases Of Trees

Growing plants under trees can be tricky, but nonetheless possible. First, you must determine how deep the the surface roots are. Some are a foot or more deep, yet with other types of trees, they are barely under the soil. In fact, you'll often see the roots popping out in various places.

Trees with roots that are close to the surface are the most difficult. The tree is much stronger than plants and will take most of the soil nutrients. The only plants that I've found to survive in this situation are those with very shallow roots. Two such ground covers are Scotch Moss and Baby Tears. Surface-rooted ferns like the Sword Fern adapt if there is sufficient moisture. This also applies to the ground covers. Enough moisture could mean watering every day to every five days, depending on the humidity and heat levels as well as on the moisture retention ability of the soil.

One plant that survives in the shade with shallow rooted trees and even during a drought is the Spider Plant. Ask your nursery about other shallow rooted plants conducive to your climate zone.

Deeper rooted trees, such as the Eucalyptus shown in the photo on the left, allow more types of plants to flourish. Sword Ferns and Elephant Leaf Philodendron, *Philodendron selloum* (zones 9 and 10), are directly under the tree with *Bougainvillea* (zones 9 and 10), in the background.

Azaleas and Rhododendrons have a special affinity for oak trees if they provide enough shade. Don't throw away the oak leaves when they fall. Put them under the plants. They provide nutrients as they decompose.

Pine trees are deep rooted and allow plants to flourish at their base as shown in the bottom photo. The original stainless steel sculpture is entitled, "Introversion".

Windsongs—A Fifth Dimension For Your Garden

The bell structure in the photo on page 104 is an original sculpture by the world famous artist, Paolo Soleri, who built the architecturally unusual commune in the desert north of Phoenix, called "Arcosanti."

His bells are fitting for a natural scene because of their crude modern design. The bronze castings produce an enthralling, mellow sound. Commercial versions of Soleri's bells in many designs are available at some art/craft galleries. If you can't locate any, call the artist's studios for the source nearest you: 1-602-948-6145.

Bells and wind chimes of the more rugged or rustic designs add an enchanting dimension to a natural garden. Soleri's bells are very heavy and require a substantial wind to make them chime. Many wind chimes will ring in soft breezes.

The wind chime in the photo on the left has a small cast iron bell in the center and is surrounded by hollow bamboo sections of various lengths.

In the Orient and South Pacific, natives make xylophone-type musical instruments from hollow bamboo. This wind chime produces similar soft mellow tones compatible to a gentle garden setting.

Rustic looking chimes are attractive when hung from tree limbs. Study your location until you find a spot that seems to get more regular breezes than others for the most enjoyment from your chimes.

The Mystique Of Arbors

Humans have had an eternal fascination with arbors. Early drawings and literature from ancient Greece and Egypt illustrate and discuss arbors. Still today, most arbors are simple wood structures with lattice or slat roofs covered with flowering vines or grapes.

The one covering a stairway in the photo on the left was made by forming an arch with heavy steel wire. Bougainvillaea branches were wrapped around the wire. If a person does not examine this arbor closely, it appears to be formed naturally by the plants. Children particularly are lured by this arbor, perhaps because it creates a tunnel.

Before building an arbor, give careful consideration to the size and location. It has to fit the flow of the landscape design, otherwise it will stick out like a sore thumb. If it is to be a large arbor, try to camouflage it with plants so it is not obvious until a person is nearly underneath it.

If your property is small, a short arbor over a garden gate may be your best choice. Climbing roses or flowering vines will give it an alluring appeal.

The bottom photo is a view from the other end of this eight foot long arbor. Boughs of magenta Bougainvillaea dance in the foreground.

One of my philosophies in creating a natural garden is that it should be a getaway from the concrete-paved environment where many of us spend a good portion of our life—a resort perhaps.

Therefore, the garden should not only be beautiful but offer many opportunities to enjoy it in other ways. Intimate little nooks and shady spots for reading and relaxing are one of the ways this can be accomplished. If you have a large property, you can probably create several such hideaways.

In the photo, the small purple flowering plant is a Lily Turf, *Liriope muscari* (zones 6 through 10). The large plant to the right is a Fairy Duster.

Before finalizing the design of any microscene, consider it from every angle. Will it look good from the north, south, east and west—if you have that many viewpoints? Of course, the view from one direction may be the best, but it should also be pleasing from other angles.

If you and your guests always see the garden from the same angle, it will lose some of its excitement and appeal. You can overcome this by making a path to a bench that invites one to enjoy the view from that spot.

Flagstone steps lead to a rustic, wood-slab bench in the top photo. If you are using open-grained wood for benches such as shown in both photos, weathering will open the grain more and allow dirt to collect which will soil clothes. Both of these benches have been lavishly coated with a clear epoxy resin to make them easy to wipe off. Epoxy resin may be obtained from fiberglass or plastic retailers and boat supply firms.

The bench in the bottom photo was made from a large tree stump with slabs of wood screwed to the top as seats. The flowering plants from top left to right are yellow Tickseed, Nasturtiums, Geraniums and Nasturtiums, again. Center, left to right are: yellow Jeruseleum Sage, white Alyssum, lavender Nile Lily, Chinese Bellflower, *Abutilon hybridum* (zones 8 through 10), and New Zealand Flax, *Phormium tenax 'Purpureum'* (zones 9 and 10).

Islands In The Sun Or Shade

A flat lawn is not very natural looking and is restrictive to the designer. Most good landscape designers will make mounds and rolling knolls to eliminate the linear, symmetrical feeling a flat lawn purveys.

Also, the unimaginative put flowers or shrubs around the perimeter of their property and leave the center to a flat, blank lawn. Of course, this means that you can mow in a straight line, but you have a boring garden.

If you want a natural look, break up the concrete sidewalks and use flagstone to make the paths meander—no straight lines. Then create some islands with soil or boulders as shown in the photos. Stone yards usually have a variety of colors and shapes—and they deliver. The cost for soil (to make mounds) or for boulders is about the same.

In both photos, a Japanese Black Pine is the center piece surrounded by a variety of exotic, clumping grasses. These grasses were chosen because they usually don't get much bigger than shown or can be cut back.

Of course, you can use flowers but be careful to find out how big everything will get when mature, otherwise the rocks will disappear and will have been a waste. In rock gardens, small plants always look the best.

A Waterfall Can Be Added To Your Pool Easily!

Nothing is more soothing and peaceful than a waterfall or a babbling brook. And for a natural landscape, what could be more apropos? What's more, a waterfall and even a brook can be added to your pool with only a couple of hours of plumbing.

In the normal operation of a pool, the water is pumped out of the pool, through a filter and then pumped back into the pool. Well, instead of returning the water to the pool by its normal route, the water is pumped to the beginning of the waterfall.

That was exactly what was done with the pool shown in the photo. In fact, the water is pumped to the beginning of a brook 30 feet from the waterfall and allowed to cascade down and over the waterfall into the pool. The plumbing costs were only $200.

If you have a flat yard, the beginning of the brook must be elevated, but as long as the brook drops an inch every five or six feet, the water will flow smoothly. First, a reinforced concrete bottom must be poured for the brook. Then, the rocks are cemented on top of the concrete.

Before you hire a stone mason, visit some shallow brooks or streams that have visible rocks and boulders. Study how the rocks are placed for a natural look and take some photos.

Generally, stone masons may not be very creative, so you may have to show him where to place the rocks. If you can find a Japanese stone mason, he may have experience building natural brooks. Check with any Japanese-owned nurseries. They might know someone.

To add more drama to the waterfall, have the mason use flagstone as ramps for the water to spill into the pool as shown in the photo.

The fun begins when the brook and waterfall are finished. Then you get to create natural settings along the sides.

Trees on the banks of the brook aren't a must, but they might make it look more natural, depending on the design of the areas adjacent to the brook. Choose slow growing trees that don't get huge when they mature. Those that become bushy and spread more horizontally are better than the trees that are lean and narrow in shape. Use several varieties with different color tones, textures and leaf shapes for more visual interest.

Beware of Weeping Willows. They have the ideal appearance for a brook, but are shallow-rooted. Their roots could lift and break the concrete base of your brook. There are several other trees with weeping branches that are not shallow rooted, such as Weeping Birch or Weeping Mulberry. They are hardy in most zones except desert areas.

For the most natural look on the banks of the brook, use a long grass. Creeping Red Fescue is shown in the photos. A few exotic clumping grasses such as Mondo Grass, Lily Turf or Blue Fescue will provide more visual interest. In a sunny spot, a Day Lily will be apropos and adds some color. Be sure to add some driftwood to the brook as well as along the banks.

The tall plant with the frilly top in the bottom photo is *Cyperus papyrus* (zones 9 and 10), more commonly known as the Paper Plant. It is a native to the banks of the Nile River in Egypt. Humans made the first paper from this plant. It needs a lot of moisture and will even grow submerged in water. In this photo, it is growing in a buried pot that doesn't have a drainage hole, to conserve the moisture it needs.

Ponds Are Easy To Make And Inexpensive

Several suppliers of pond materials advertise in gardening magazines. Essentially, they are selling butyl plastic pond liners. To make a pond, you simply dig a hole in any shape you want, line it with the butyl and use sod and stones to cover the liner where it emerges from the pond.

You don't need a filter, pump or aerator unless you plan to add fish such as koi or goldfish. There is a fish that is a must that doesn't require aeration. That's the Mosquito Fish which eats mosquito larvae. They are free from your local mosquito abatement district or park service. In some areas, you can call them and they will deliver the fish. You don't have to feed these tiny fish, since they live on the larvae.

The pond in the photo is above ground in the center of a paved motor court in front of a house. It has a clover leaf shaped rigid fiberglass liner and a stone and brick exterior. The fountain (shown in the photo on this page) forms a fleur-de-lis pattern. A miniature sunken ship's rigging appears in the front edge of pond in this photo.

Along with the water lilies are water irises on the right and cattails behind the original kinetic stainless steel sculpture entitled, "Windribbons."

The most natural walkways are simply beaten paths, but they present several negative aspects. They get muddy and require weeding. Fine gravel is the next choice, but still needs weeding, gets mushy when wet and guests' shoes get scuffed.

The best choice is flagstone for the most natural appearance. Grass or other ground covers can be allowed to grow in between. The opposite photo shows Baby Tears growing between the stones in this shaded area.

An alternative to ground covers between the flagstone is small round pebbles as shown in the photo on this page. Be sure to press the pebbles down so that they are slightly below the flagstone, otherwise they will be kicked out as the walk is used.

A path is man's intrusion into nature, so it is okay to show that this intrusion is man-made. We've shown that sculptures, statues, bridges, gazebos and garden ornaments add visual interest and don't destroy the natural appearance.

Therefore, any man-made substance can be used as long as it is rustic, rugged and not done in a straight line. In the opposite photo is an inexpensive yet quaint approach.

Tile layers and tile shops throw out a lot of broken tile—especially the cheap clay ones. The ones in the photo on your left are Mexican clay paver tiles which were broken in shipment and received free from a tile layer. The ones that were only chipped were intentionally broken to maintain the rustic appearance of the path. Notice how it meanders, contradicting the straight edges of the tile.

In the photo below, a combination of used common brick and irregular pieces of two colors of flagstone were laid in an intentionally inconsistent pattern.

Building Around Nature

If you are planning on building a house or adding on to an existing one, there is one thing that you should consider—building around any existing trees. This makes your intrusion upon nature less obvious, allows the landscape and structure to flow together more naturally and adds a dramatic flair that is appreciated by all who view it.

The guest house in the opposite photo was built within three feet of a 30-foot high Japanese Black Pine. The branch hanging down was fiercely protected during the construction because it is such a great design element. Other branches (not shown) also dip down below the roof line further enhancing the natural feeling of the setting.

Avoid Borders When Possible

Borders add a linear look which is best avoided whenever possible in a natural garden. However, when microscenes adjoin a lawn that you mow, you have only two choices. One, make the edge of the lawn meander and don't use any wood, metal or plastic border edging. This makes mowing more difficult, but a gas or electric edger cuts the grass very effectively where it can't be reached with a mower.

The second choice is to just allow the grass to grow underneath the plants unmowed. If you are using a low growing ground cover that grows sideways as shown in the bottom photo, there's no problem.

How To Give An Average Scene More Appeal

For a moment, imagine the scene on the right without the statue of a Pan. When analyzed, it is not particularly interesting. But by adding the statue, the area's visual impact is enhanced.

I included this photo to show the design value of the right garden ornaments. Actually, this picture was taken in early spring before the appearance of several late-rising herbacious perennials which do make it more interesting. The annuals, white and purple Alyssum, and a poppy were sown in the fall to make sure this area was not bland in spring.

All Microscenes Need A Focal Point

The abstract statue of a woman's head in the photo below was added to put a focal point in this scene. For a microscene to be considered an appealing design, it must have a focal point.

The scene on the left is another that needed a focal point. The soil on this slope limited the choice of plants, and therefore it needed something for visual impact, supplied by the original bronze sculpture. The floating flowerheads from a cactus seem to be exotic snakes charmed by the flute of "The Shaman."

The same applies to the scene on this page. This statue can be made by anyone handy with a table saw. This is a miniature modernized rendition of the ancient Hindu and Buddist pagodas still maintained throughout Asia. Many of them have multitiered towers. Japanese garden artisans make replicas like these from stone or concrete. They are available commercially, but they are expensive.

This one was made from 2x12 redwood with one-half inch pieces recessed between tiers. Each of the lower tiers are one-eighth inch smaller as they rise and the edges are angled in slightly.

A Way To Expand Your Design Area

The size of the plants you use often restricts the number and arrangement of the plants in a microscene. The old standby, "a low row in front, a medium-height row in the middle and a tall row in back," usually doesn't look natural, and doesn't allow design freedom.

One way to overcome this is to build planter boxes higher and wider than usual—three-feet high and deep. Used railroad ties can be stacked to make planters in irregular shapes. Even islands can be created.

In the photo below, a problem embankment was made more useful with three tiers of planter terraces. Although redwood was used in this situation, generally railroad ties are better, because they won't rot. Ask your lumber dealer or nursery where you can buy used ties locally.

The photo on the left shows another view of the same terraces. The purple flower (in front of the original bronze sculpture, "Cyberena") is Sea Lavender. The pink and white flowers are Sweet William. The red flowers in the photo below are Cannas—a perennial that blooms for several months (all zones except in 4 to 7, where they must be dug up before winter and replanted in the spring).

Specially For The West And Southwest

If you live significantly east of the Rocky Mountains, a desert scene in your area would certainly be incongruous; but in the west, deserts abound.

In many places, the only plants that will grow without extensive amendment of the soil are desert plants. That was the case with the scene on the opposite page, except soil amendment didn't help.

The keys to making a desert scene interesting are a variety of different shaped plants with some boulders and sun-bleached driftwood or saguaro logs. In this scene, the driftwood was added for erosion control due to the slope. A large live Saguaro would be a great centerpiece, but because they grow so slowly, they are very expensive.

For those who have never been in a desert in the spring, many desert plants flower—and some quite handsomely. In the middle far right of the photo, the orange flower belong to the Coral Aloe, *Aloe striata* (zones 9 and 10). This cactus is one of the earliest bloomers, and its blossoms last for about a month.

The original stainless steel sculpture shown in the photo is entitled, "Love Knot".

The Most Natural Lawn And You Mow It

Every Five Years!

"You're dreaming!" you say. *"There must be a catch."* No. I'm not dreaming. The Korean Velvet Grass, shown in the photo on your right, has only one limitation. It's not hardy if the temperature stays below 20 degrees F, for any substantial length of time.

I'm sorry about that, my northern friends, but the southerners in zones 8 through 10 can rejoice. The reason you have to cut it so seldomly is that it grows sideways. The only maintenance is edging it once or twice a year. In a few years, it would completely cover up a walk or small boulder if you didn't edge it.

If you have flagstone walks like those shown in the photo, you don't have to edge around them. Just make a couple of cuts in the flap of grass growing over them, pull the flagstone out, put soil or sand in the hole it left and lay the flagstone back down. The same applies to boulders—and you only have to do this once a year.

This is really a tough grass. It can take foot traffic which just slows down the growth where you walk regularly. In the photo, you can see that the grass seems shorter around the flagstone.

The grass in this photo and the one on the next page has not been cut for four years. By the third year, it is thick with an irregular or bumpy surface, but it is fun to walk or lie on because it is springy or spongy. Cats and dogs think it is strange and prefer to use the flagstone or walks, but kids love to play and roll around on it.

By the fourth year, it will be a foot thick in spots where it hits an obstruction as shown by the ruler in the photo on the opposing page. By the fifth year, the grass is too thick and begins separating showing the dried grass underneath. So finally, it is time to mow the thick areas. You'll need a heavy duty, 5 H.P. rotary mower. Anything less will not do the job. Many gardening companies use large mowers like these.

Korean Velvet Grass, *Zoysia tenuifolia*, is very drought resistant and about twice as expensive as the best sod. It comes in flats which you cut into two-inch squares and plant about three inches apart as shown in the photo on this page. It takes this grass one growing season to fill in between the plugs.

After the first year, you must fertilize it every three months during the growing season, or it will get yellow. This grass goes dormant in the fall for three or four months, but stays green if you don't get a heavy frost.

Grass Doesn't Really Need Mowing Anyway!

That statement certainly goes against conventional thinking, but let's examine it. Grass in a natural wild setting doesn't get mowed, does it? The grass in the photo to the left hasn't been mowed in 10 years! I'm sure you will agree that it looks natural and pleasant.

Tall grass like this gets a windswept tousled look that many people find appealing. This grass is called Creeping Red Fescue. I don't know why they call it "red" because I've never detected any red in it. It is an annual grass, but it reseeds intensively with almost invisible seeds.

Late in the fall every year, it is raked with a sharp tooth rake to pull out the dried old grass. The only care given is regular watering and feeding. Since the grass is longer than a mowed lawn, obviously it needs more water and food to maintain its health.

This fescue, *Festuca rubra*, survives well in zones 4 to 10. However, there are similar grasses available in all zones. Some require that you reseed every spring, but in many cases, no extensive soil preparation is required. Discuss the grasses available in your area with a local nursery.

Enjoying Your Landscape Indoors

After you have created an awesome natural garden, you'll want to enjoy viewing it as much as possible. Surely, you must have made microscenes that can be seen from the living room, dining room, kitchen and master bedroom. The photo below was taken from a dining room and the view certainly adds to the romance of dining.

Unfortunately, many homes have small windows in most rooms that restrict the view. If that is your situation, this might be the time to consider doing a little remodeling by replacing some of those windows with larger ones. It would probably improve the value of your home. If you are planning to build, tell the architect what you have in mind for the garden.

As a reader of this book, you probably have lots of plants in your home. Most indoor plants are native to the tropics with its hot and steamy climate. There's one place in your house that has the same climate, at least for a while each day—your bathroom. The bathroom in the photo on the opposite page shows one way to capitalize on the environment of the sunken tub/shower combination.

Landscape architects and designers begin creating a plan for a garden with a scale drawing of your land. Then they draw circles in each plant's proposed location scaled to the equivalent diameter of the mature size of the plant.

If you have a small lot, this may seem like an unnecessary technical process, but it will save aggravation later. The aggravation will be the sweat and strain of digging up and moving plants that have grown too large for the spot where they were located.

If you are going to create only a couple of microscenes, you can use a can of white spray paint to paint circles on the ground. I use this technique to locate the center of the holes to be dug. A drawing, of course, is much superior for planning.

Before drawing the circles for the plants, use a highlighting marker pen and color the areas that are shaded for most of the day—10 A.M. to 7 P.M. Use a different colored marker for the parts of your garden that are partially shaded for more than half of the day.

As you probably know, there are plants that prefer full sun, those that tolerate partial shade and ones that do well in full shade. Don't ignore the plants' preferences. If you do, the plants will either die or perform very poorly.

Now you are ready to begin choosing plants for thevarious scenes you are about to create. There is a book entitled, *Color Encyclopedia of Garden Plants and Habitats* by Fritz Kohlein and Peter Menzel, published by Timber Press, that covers the most common flowering plants and clumping grasses. This book specifies the U.S.D.A. zones for each plant. If your local bookstore doesn't have it, they can order it for you.

That book doesn't cover trees and shrubs, but there's one that is found in many libraries which is very comprehensive, entitled *Trees and Shrubs: A Complete Guide* by Richard Gorer. Check bookstores as there may be books on the trees that grow in your particular region that will save you a lot of reading.

If you live in the states west of the Rocky Mountains, there is a second book that every gardener should have. It is the *Sunset Western Garden Book*, published by *Sunset Magazine*. This is the bible for western gardeners, and in fact, you'll find a heavily used copy in every nursery.

This garden book has broken down the 10 U.S.D.A. zones, which are very general, into 24 more specific zones that cover a lot of microclimates caused by the variable terrain common in the western states.

The *Sunset* book goes further than most plant encyclopedias. With the description of each plant, tree or shrub, they give helpful hints about each plant's idiosnycracies. Although this book covers practically anything that will grow in the western states, there are no color pictures of the plants—just illustrations.

Unfortunately, no one publishes a similar book for plants east of the Rockies. The *Sunset* book is available in all bookstores and many nurseries in the west.

There is an important final tip you should remember in choosing plants for each microscene. Pick plants that flower at different times of the year, so you will have color in each scene throughout the growing season.

All On Two-Thirds Of An Acre!

All of the photographs on the previous pages in this book were taken two-thirds of an acre of land! There are over 800 plants, shrubs and trees on about one-half of the acre because the house, guest house, garage, driveway and paved motor court take up one-third of the land.

The aerial photos show the property lines. Due to the contours of the land and numerous trees, there is no one spot where you can see all parts of the property, giving it a much larger feeling.

The reason I am presenting the book this way is to show you how numerous microscenes can be joined together seamlessly to create a spectacular garden. You'll see the before and after photos on the following pages.

When this house was purchased, there was a small run-down house and a virtual jungle of vines, briars, brush and various non-specimen type trees. Nine tons of overgrowth and vines were removed along with 40 trees of various sizes—22 mature trees were left.

The before photo below shows how it looked after all the vegetation was removed. Several trees in this photo were subsequently removed including the two in the foreground.

A Japanese style guest house, called the "Teahouse" was built on the corner and used as a library, office and art studio. You can see a number of the microscenes, shown earlier, in the photo to your left.

Pool Area Landscaping

The before photo below shows the area where the pool is now before any vegetation was removed. A concrete block retaining wall separated the slope from the yard. It was removed to allow the flat area to flow more naturally into the slope by mounding soil up a few feet from the base level. All the trees in this area were removed because they did not fit into the overall design plan.

The brook was cut diagonally across the slope to increase its length before reaching the waterfall as you can see in the after photo. Brooks are such great design elements that the longer you can let one run, the more opportunities you have for microscenes.

There are eight of the microscenes shown in previous pages in the after photo. Can you find them?

Here are views of the southeast corner of the property. The ugly concrete block wall is the southern property line and was hidden with a tall redwood fence covered with reed. The grey-toned tree in the right foreground was left and the hot tub deck built around it. This tree forms a naturally fitting canopy over the deck as you will see in the photo on page 162. A small viewing deck was built in the upper corner of the property as you can see in the after photo because this spot provides the best overview of much of the entire garden.

You'll probably notice that the garden appears much larger in the after photos on the previous page and to the right. The photographer's perspective is somewhat different in each, which contributes partially to the difference. The primary reason is that in the before photos, the walls confine and delineate the property. In the after photos, the delineation is removed so that the base of the yard continues to flow up the slope as one. This is a basic principle of "natural" garden design: don't delineate unless you have to, and if you have to, then use the line or wall as a design element.

This property is essentially two one-half acre lots on two levels. The upper level is unevenly sloped and impractical as a building site. This level is about 100 feet wide and rises 26 feet from the bottom lot—pretty steep!

The soil on the upper level was thin, averaging about four inches deep, sandy and was almost infertile. Under the soil is a conglomorate of rocks nearly cemented together. Extensive soil amendment was done, and the holes for all plants were dug twice the normal size and filled with fresh soil to provide a sufficient nutrient base.

Both photos are views of the center section of the northern half of the property. Several trees were planted into the steepest part of the lower slope. The retaining wall was removed and a rolling earth berm made the transition from flat area to steep slope not as noticable. The overall design effect of these techniques is obvious in the after photo on the page to your left.

In both photos, we are looking toward the back yard from the front of the house. A portion of the retaining wall survived here and was covered with stone as a design element.

A stone planter was added where the yard widened near the front of the house. The dining room, with floor to ceiling windows, looks out onto this planter. That was the reason it was put there, since beyond that, the steep embankment didn't offer much opportunity to put on a display of plants and flowers. The view from the dining room was shown on page 143.

The old house was torn down to the foundation and a much larger redwood-clad house built over and beyond the old foundation. In most sections of the house, large expanses of glass provide panoramic garden views.

Eight Microscenes

These photos were taken of the northwest corner of the property. The before photo shows one of the many loads of brush and vines ready for removal. Two laborers spent three weeks removing the unsightly vegetation. A crew of four tree men spent nearly a week removing 40 trees. But as you can see in the end result, it was worth it.

Eight of the microscenes shown in the previous pages are visible in this photograph. Notice how they all flow together.

The Teahouse has a large deck where the view includes the ocean, and looking down, we see the main house and pool garden in the photo on your right.

The tree around which the hot tub was built around was pruned so it would have a canopy like an unbrella. This is a River Wattle, *Acacia subperosa* (zones 8 through 10), which has long thin draping branches much like a Weeping Willow Tree. The umbrella effect was accomplished by removing many of the interior branches.

Below is a closeup of the far end of the pool. If you are wondering if a flock of ducks just happened to drop in, the answer is no. These are authentic-looking hand-painted decoys. At first, you might think that putting decoys in a pool is corny, but with this natural setting, this quirky addition is fitting. Cats and dogs are fascinated by the ducks as the breeze causes them to move around.

Capitalize On Your Best Viewing Spot

The photo to your left was taken from a small viewing deck (shown in the photo on page 155) which gives a panorama of much of the property. Here you can see the effect of using different colored trees, various plant foliage shapes and textures to keep every view interesting—even without flowers.

At the corner of the house, a spiral staircase and a roof deck were added when we discovered that the roof offered more fascinating views. The deck is blocked by a tree in this photo but can be seen on the previous page. The deck is popular with the family as well as guests, as it offers a choice of broad views of the the garden and often, of spectacular sunsets.

The pool was designed to look more like a pond with boulders along its edges. An overhanging willow would appear to be a perfect choice for a tree by this pool, but when the size was considered, I decided it would block a part of the garden view from the patio. Instead, the large Japanese Black Pine, which is growing horizontally, is just as naturally appealing without obstructing the view.

Paths Stimulate Curiosity

The photo on your left was taken from the upper fence line, beside the Teahouse, looking down toward the lower level.

As you can see, paths trail off in every direction. On a large landscape with many microscenes, paths are important for two reasons. Of course, from a practical standpoint, paths allow maintenance with minimal damage from trampling. Of more importance, you can design pathways to control the views of people walking through your garden. Also, a path will cause people to investigate, out of curiosity, where it leads.

Often, Japanese garden designers make paths that zigzag, causing visitors to slow down and focus on important scenes. It is a very effective technique because a walk through a garden should be slow and deliberate, allowing your senses to absorb all the beautiful details.

Killed Two Problem Birds With 26 Tons Of Stone!

The photo on the left is a partial view of the northeast quadrant of the property from the upper center to the Teahouse.

The laborers digging the holes for hundreds of plants on this hillside wore out two posthole diggers and broke three shovels on the rocky substrata below the thin top soil.

The problem was what to do with the tons of rock we were accumulating. At the base of the upper level is a concrete swale, a ditch made to carry water runoff to prevent erosion. It's two feet wide and a foot deep and certainly would be ugly in a natural landscape.

I decided to kill two problem birds with 26 tons of stone. We put all the rock we were accumulating in the swale and created a 209 foot long natural-looking dry stream. You can see it alongside the path in the photo.

The flowers in the photo on this page are Spineless Safflowers.

The photo on this page was taken looking in the opposite direction from the one on the previous page. This is the northwest quadrant. The variety of plants on this rugged hillside imbues the feeling that it always looked this way. Again, I'll point out that variety in size, shape, color and texture are the vital keys to creating a fascinating, natural landscape, as you can see here.

The wooden structure in the center is a stylized light—part of the outdoor lighting system. These are subtle lights that provide just enough illumination to outline various scenes, and so that you can see to walk around on moonless nights. A balmy evening walk through your garden can be as enjoyable as in the daylight. It's a different feeling—more exotic and mysterious. An alfresco candlelight dinner in a gazebo can be even more romantic than the most alluring restaurant in town.

The photo on the left was lit entirely by the ordinary pool lights under the water. This enthralling view is a focal point from many parts of the house at night.

Every day for a certain period of time, I have a rainbow in my garden—if the sun is shining—and so can you. Adults love it, and children are absolutely overwhelmed and want to find the pot of gold.

The rainbow in the photo was created by a special sprinkling system that I designed for my potted bonsai trees. Potted bonsai must be watered daily during the summer months because the small amount of soil in their pots dries out quickly. Overhead sprinkler systems, however, produce big droplets of water which tend to wash the soil out of the pots.

My solution for this problem is misting sprinkler heads pointed straight up. You can see them just above the ground cover in front of the bonsai trees. These misting heads shoot up a column of mist about seven feet high. Obviously, as the sun shines through the mist, a rainbow results.

Put one in your garden. It's great entertainment for family and friends. It doesn't take much talent to make one. The parts just screw together. Mount four or five misting heads on a section of PVC pipe, then attach it it to your garden hose. Or you can make a permanent installation by burying it and attaching it to your sprinkler system.

As You Leave Earthsong...

For those who truly appreciate and love nature, there is nothing so peaceful and serene as a richly vibrant natural setting.

For those who work in bustling cities, to come home to a beautiful garden is to escape from the harsh artificiality of the metropolis—a very personal retreat.

Nature attracts nature, so a special garden, with a large variety of God's best vegetation, will attract songful birds and flitting butterflies who are also looking for a safe retreat. And you'll be rewarded by their presence since the folks without gardens will rarely see them.

Although a magnificient garden will improve the value of your home, the wealth of pleasure you'll obtain from it is very hard to buy.

As we leave Earthsong, I hope that I have given you some ideas and direction so you can make your own patch of earth sing with natural beauty.

Photography

The candid photograph of the author taking a cool shot in the pool was taken by his wife, Annette Revel, with a 35mm Canon camera, 50mm lens and Kodacolor 100 film.

The aerial photographs on page 148 were taken by Aerial Photo Service, San Francisco, California.

The balance of the photographs were taken by the author with a Mamiya RZ67 medium-format camera using a variety of lenses from 50mm to 200mm. The source of light was natural in all cases except for the night scene which was lit with ordinary underwater pool lights. Fuji transparency film, Velvia and Provia, were used for most of the shots. Some color print film was used, which was Kodacolor 100.

Sculptures

Wherever the text indicates a sculpture is original, it was done by the author with the exception of Paolo Soleri's untitled bell sculpture on page 106.

Acknowledgments

All scientific facts in this book were verified by Bas Mulder, who earned his M.S. degree in horticulture at the Agricultural University of Wageningen in the Netherlands. Mr. Mulder also has over 10 years experience as a landscape architect and designer. He owns the design firm, BM Design in Los Angeles, and is the chief horticulturist for Sassafras Nursery in Topanga, California.

The private garden featured in this book is located in Pacific Palisades, California.

Sources

PLANT AND TREE CATALOGS:

Wayside Gardens
1 Garden Lane
Hodges, SC 29695-0001
(Trees and Perennials)

Henry Fields Nursery Co.
415 North Burnett
Shenandoah, Iowa 51602
(Trees and Perennials)

Milaeger's Gardens
4838 Douglas Avenue
Racine, Wisconsin 53424
(Perennials)

Van Bourgondien Nurseries
245 Farmingdale Road
Babylon, New York 11702-0598
(Perennials and Bulbs)

BOOKS:

"The American Horticultural Society Encyclopedia
of Garden Plants"
MacMillillan Publishing Co.
ISBN 0-02-557920-7

"The Encyclopedia of Ornamental Grasses"
Michael Friedman Publishing Group
ISBN 0-87596-100-2

"Sunset Western Garden Book"
Sunset Publishing Corp.
ISBN 0-376-03891-8

Index